MW01200482

Published by Jovial Press

ISBN-13: 978-1537209975

ISBN-10: 1537209973

THE LAY OF REDEMPTION

Joseph Carlson

Publisher's Foreword

It is entirely possible that everything that we deem most important is mistaken. We are surrounded by state-of-the-art technologies, untested ideas, new poetic and artistic forms and mediums, and cutting edge forms of communication for all of them. None of this is a bad thing in itself. Every thing is new at some point. But it turns out that being human is a generational exercise. We learn from those that have gone before us in order to have wisdom for our own generation. Our triumphs and failures are the fodder of the next generation's search for the wisdom. But with such extensive newness on every side, our generation is simply the guinea pig of history.

Into this *experimentum novum* comes the poetry of Joseph Carlson. I am a fan of Joseph Carlson. His poetry, his writing, his person. I am a fan. I get excited when I get new poetry from him. But I also believe that his poetry is good for the modern soul. In his unashamed embrace of old forms Carlson reinvigorates something deeply human that, in our pursuit of the newest flash of shine, we have willingly laid aside. In his imagistic and rhythmic reminders of our history, Carlson pulls back together the fragments of our soul that we have shattered in our pursuit of new and robotic efficiencies.

The Lay of Redemption is a poem to come back to over and over. Whenever you need to be reminded of the beauty of the plan of redemption, to be de-gnosticized back into the historical faith of the Christian story, then Carlson's poetry is what you need. If you have this poem on your shelf then you will always know where to go to have the dust blown from your memory.

Jason Farley — Jovial Hall; August, 2016

Introduction

This is a work of poetic theology. It is a theological treatise on typology, fulfillment, the literary nature of the Bible, the beauty and genius of Holy Spirit as Author, the consistency of His narrative, and the thread of redemption woven through the whole, from the garden of Eden to the garden of the empty tomb. However, unlike most of the books on poetic theology available today, this is actually a poem. As such, I hope to communicate truth, not only in what is written, but also in how it is written.

I desire to reimagine with you the specific story of redemption traced through key figures in the Old Testament, culminating in the person of Jesus. In the garden, within minutes after the Fall, God promised salvation to Adam and Eve. The seed of the woman would crush the head of the serpent. From that point on there is a single thread woven through every chapter, every verse, every story of the Old Testament. That thread is the coming Messiah. All points to Him. All anticipates Him. Jesus, whose very name means God will save, is concealed on every page of the Hebrew Scriptures. And when Matthew opens the New Testament and shows us the son of David, the son of Abraham, everything that came before finally falls into place with the satisfaction that comes when the last piece of the puzzle smoothly joins the whole together and reveals something beautiful.

That is the goal of this work—to explore and discover Jesus through the characters and types in the Old Testament. Seven shadows, all pointing to one Person. To this end, each section is titled three ways: A Day—A Man—A Virtue. The day represents one of the days of creation; the man is the main character of that section; and the virtue is the dominant theme. The successive days of creation (their individual themes are interwoven with the narrative of each day) hint at the world being formed and shaped in anticipation of the Seed of the Woman. The first seven men all point to Jesus as types or shadows. The virtues define each of the men in a particular way, with all of them finding complete fullness in Jesus.

My hope is that, when you get to Day Eight, you will notice how Jesus wraps everything up. He is that final puzzle piece that brings complete and final satisfaction. You might notice how seven of the stanzas in that section reference the characteristics of the days of creation, and the attributes described in the seven preceding sections. If you do, the intention there is to proclaim that in Christ, the world is being made new. After God "unmade" the world through the prophets (detailed in the third interlude), He recreates it in Jesus. And he that sat upon the throne said, Behold, I make all things new (Revelation 21:5). This is our only hope in this world, that we be found in Christ, and made new by His Spirit. His sacrifice opened the door for us to die with Him by faith, so that we might also be buried with Him by faith, and be raised with Him to newness of life by faith. Therefore believe on Him! Come before the throne of Jesus and worship Him above all gods. *For God also hath highly exalted him, and given him a name which is above every name: That at the name of Jesus every knee should bow, of things in heaven, and things in earth, and things under the earth; And that every tongue should confess that Jesus Christ is Lord, to the glory of God the Father* (Philippians 2:9-11).

My central goal in this work is to bring glory and honor to the name of Jesus. He Himself is living Truth; He alone is Good; He is the ultimate standard and expression of Beauty. To put it another way, we must come before Him and worship. Augustine, in his great work on the Trinity said this:

> [We do not bear] the image of God, because the mind remembers itself, and understands and loves itself, but because it can also remember, understand, and love Him by whom it was made. And in so doing it becomes wise. But if it does not do so, even when it remembers, understands, and loves itself, then it is foolish. Let us

then remember our God, after whose image we are made, and let us understand and love Him. Or to say the same thing more briefly, let us worship God, who is not made, by whom we were made... wherefore it is written, "Behold, the worship of God, that is wisdom." And in this we will be wise, not by our own light, but by participation of that supreme Light. (On the Trinity, Book XIV, chapter 12)

My desire in this poem is to offer you a remembering of who we are, what this world is, our need of Jesus, and the perfections of the Christ. The goal of memory is understanding, and the goal of understanding is love. This love drives us to worship. And here is the beginning of wisdom. Each of us must drop to our knees before the risen King in love and adoration, worshipping His holy name.

THE LAY OF
REDEMPTION

Proem

Once more O Muse, lift up your voice and sing!
Bright Heaven's Bard, inspire our hearts, grown cold.
Your holy fire of Truth and Goodness bring
That songs of Beauty may again be told.
Our weak imaginations have grown old
And lost the will to wonder at Your song.
Ignite in us the courage to be bold!
Our feet of clay stand shaking on the strong
Forgotten shoulders of the saints we wrong.

Our idle minds, amused and underfed —
Not from a lack of food, but lack of heart —
Must be reshaped by Gospel wine and bread,
To see ourselves as children set apart
From worldly ways, shaped by a different art.
The story of man reconciled to God,
Redemption songs, O Muse, now take your part.
We pray that we may see from fathers flawed
The Beauty of the Christ whose name we laud.

Day One—Adam—Maturity

Of earth's first days I have already sung;
How unheard mirth and love were woven tight
Into the fabric of a world so young,
How words of pow'r took shape—and there was light.
Six mornings did the Maker use to write
His character into creation's frame;
Six evenings etched a benediction bright
Upon the living words with setting flame;
To bring creation rest, a seventh came.

The world was full of life—each blade of grass,
Each beam of light dispelling dark night's cloud,
The trees, the teeming seas and all that passed
Along its paths, the mountain peaks unbowed,
The fertile fields where horse and oxen proud
Roamed free beneath the sun—all words of life
The Maker's mirth in pow'r had sung aloud.
This world of rich abundance without strife
Was given to God's son and to his wife.

For unknown days, an unknown innocence,
Like morning mist upon the morning air,
A light-born, living wholeness did evince.
The whole world knelt—the land, the sea—in prayer;
High gratitude for Him whose heav'nly care
Had filled each moment with inspired song
To teach the man, who did His image bear,
To reach maturity, to make him strong;
And in high Heaven's time, know right from wrong.

E'en now, each moment known the Maker makes
With meaning and intent, to shake me free
Of disbelief, my senses to awake,
And fill me full with faith, that I might see
He means each word, each sound—gives all to me
To train my ears to cherish every psalm
Creation sings; for in each harmony
The melody of grace in graceful calm
Comes straightway to my soul with healing balm.

Like darkened figs upon the autumn tree,
Which in their season drop, full ripe and sweet,
By patient art, man learns maturity.
Or like the harvesting of summer wheat,
When golden in the sun, its time complete,
Man's patient pains are brought to final rest.
Thus waiting is the first of wisdom's feats.
Maturity, time's benediction blessed,
Cannot be grasped, or without faith possessed.

So, man's first war was on this fair field fought,
And lost—in pride he seized the chance to know,
Before faith could be tried, or wisdom sought;
But knowledge without faith is poisoned woe.
Yet nothing without faith in something grows;
Thus faithlessness a faith in self implies.
So man in self did trust, and was brought low —
As low as any grave, for he must die
Who turns his faith from God in Heaven high.

The Maker's word was simple: "Build, protect,
Bring fruitfulness and beauty to a waiting land;
Embrace and keep your bride, my love reflect."
But Adam would despise God's first command.
All things were his, the whole world in his hand;
Still, not enough to satisfy the pride
That in him welled, the drive to understand
The Maker's thoughts and ways without a guide,
To stand alone, and with himself abide.

But courage too, as well as faith, he lacked.
His bride between himself and danger set,
He from a distance watched, afraid to act.
This failure to eliminate the threat
Gave way unto desire, which sin begets.
His sin, to taste forbidden fruit untried,
Cast all his race beneath the curse of sweat,
Of blood and tears and endless years denied.
The man and wife were sent away—and died.

For death is darkness, broke from living light,
A separation of what once was one.
Into this darkened, empty pit of night
Our human father fell, hid from the sun;
Hid from the light of peace that he had shunned.
And so, though many years before them lay,
And many trials before their days be done,
It was that our parents died that fateful day
They ate the fruit, and thus were sent away.

And yet, before they left that garden fair,
A promise to this darkened race was made:
A woman's child would find the dragon's lair
And bruise his head with His own blood and blade.
The woman's seed would on a cross be flayed,
His bald heel bruised, His bare arms spread out wide.
Though crucified, this brave child unafraid
Would enter Death's own mouth and from inside
That dragon slay, who kept Him from His bride.

In Him maturity would fullness find,
For He would patiently, through testing years,
Obey His Father's will, though oft maligned;
Would set His face, though racked with crippling fears,
Upon the task of conquering the tears.
As wine is only wine once grapes are pressed;
As bread is only bread when once the ears
To flour are ground—so Man would be his best
When cross-shaped faith the willing seed expressed.

Day Two—Noah—Righteousness

The world was thrown into a den of death,
As sons of fathers died, and lived no more —
Long lists of generations without breath,
The names of men who passed through Sheol's door.
But after centuries beneath time's war,
A child was born, whose father prophesied,
"Up from the clay, out of the earth's cursed floor,
This son has come and will relief provide
From all the crowns of thorns our hands have tied."

Thus Noah grew to be a righteous son
Who walked with God, unheard of in those days.
For east of Eden was with sin o'errun,
And none but Noah loved the Maker's ways.
The sons of Heaven did Earth's daughters praise,
And took as wives whomever they might choose.
Thus mighty gods were born, though, all ablaze
With lust, they craved the power to abuse
Creation, their depraved minds to amuse.

The Maker grieved. Heart-sore to see the hell
His world of beauty had so quick become.
He watched the wicked hearts of men rebel
Against His kindness as their souls turned numb.
To evil only did their minds succumb.
A stagnant sea of foul iniquity,
The Maker set His face to scrape the scum;
To blot out man and beast and all things He
Regretted now, with weeping eyes, to see.

Save Noah, who alone had faith in God.
Thus, to this blameless son, the Maker said:
"All flesh must shortly die, for men have gnawed
The living heart out of my world, now dead,
And eaten violence as if it were bread.
I will destroy them, with the earth they rape.
But you, my son, your sons and wives, instead
Shall know my grace and will my wrath escape;
Now watch as I this fallen world reshape."

That herald both of righteousness and trust
Believed the word the Maker did impart;
Assured of things unseen that would, that must,
Take place, this faith poured strength into his heart,
Made firm his mind and limbs to take his part.
For faith accepts His word, but acts as well,
And, trusting, strikes a path, a course to chart.
Faith builds within: the confidence to quell
All doubt; without: a peace in which to dwell.

Thus Noah built an ark of gopher wood,
To keep, of every kind of beast, a pair.
Though oft maligned by scoffers who withstood
With mocking words their own innate despair,
This faithful son to God alone in prayer
Took all his captive thoughts, and so was sure.
Soon came the varied host from land and air
Of clean and unclean both to dwell secure
Within the ark, God's judgment to endure.

The world was split in two—as water tore
From fountains deep, through windows in the sky.
For forty days and forty nights the door
Of every cistern emptied its supply.
The waters from below and from on high
Met in one cataclysmic flood of death;
Beneath the waves of heav'n all flesh did die.
But there within the ark, the sons of Seth
Were kept alive, baptized in life's strong Breath.

For many days they rode the wrathful sea,
While waters cleansed the earth both far and wide.
For many months, the ark of jubilee
No harbor found, but rested on the tide,
And on the Maker's mercy all relied.
Then God remembered Noah, the vow made
To him and the whole world he kept inside.
He spoke—the fountains of the deep obeyed,
And all the windows of the heav'ns were stayed.

The time had come to leave and start afresh;
A year and ten days had been spent at sea.
"Go, and with you bring all of every flesh,"
The Maker said, "that all may fruitful be,
And fill the earth again with harmony."
And it was so—they left the wooden womb;
All beasts, all birds and all that move were free
To leave the ark and life on earth resume,
As One would one day leave an empty tomb.

An altar built and sacrifices flayed,
The faithful man gave thanks unto the Lord.
The Maker's heart was moved, this promise made:
"I nevermore will curse the earth with waters poured
From heav'n, nor will I smite earth's living horde
Because of man. The seasons forth shall go;
While earth remains, all times shall be restored.
And when within the cloud you see My bow,
This promise made to you, you then will know."

Yet there will be a reckoning for man.
Whoever sheds man's blood must give his own,
For in the Maker's image we began;
So for the death of man, man must atone,
A debt that can be paid by man alone.
To pay this debt, a Son, up from the clay,
To bring relief from thorns mankind has sown,
Must come and be man's ark—the only way
To find safe harbor on that wrathful day.

Interlude—Fallen is Babel

Now, with one language all the earth did speak.
They came from realms beyond the rising sun,
And finding plains in Shinar, settled there.
"Now come," they said, "and let us build a tow'r —
To reach the heav'ns, and make for us a name
Lest we be scattered over earth's wide face."
The Lord came down to see what they had made.
"Behold," He said, "they all have joined as one
And nothing they now think will not be done.
Let us go down to see this pride displayed
To scatter them, remove them from this place,
And cool in them that self-regard inflamed."
They therefore ceased to build their ode to pow'r
When God removed them from that dragon's lair,
Dispersed them o'er the face of realms unwon,
Their language mixed, and made each tongue unique.

That half-forgotten city thence was Babel named—
The shape of man's rebellion, ever shamed.

Day Three—Abraham—Faith

Long years to generations then did flow,
As fathers still had sons in hope of rest.
The tower had fallen, and Babel's woe
Had forced them on to fill the unpossessed,
Unpeopled lands that lay to east and west.
In this mixed world a child, a son, was born.
His father named him Abram: Father Blessed.
Though irony would soon make Abram mourn;
For his wife, Sarai, wept with womb forlorn.

The Lord showed grace to Noah's distant seed
And with him spoke: "Now leave your father's clan
And kin behind and follow where I lead,
To seek a country far beyond the sand.
A fertile ground I place within your hand
To ever bless your name, your pathway pave.
For I will make of you a lasting land —
A nation set apart from raging waves.
And through your seed, all peoples I will save."

In faith, the seedless Abram journeyed west.
For faith calls true the things that are not seen,
In confidence relies on hoped-for rest,
Upon the Maker's Word has learned to lean —
A faith that sees the wastelands growing green.
This son of faith, foresaw a faith-born son,
His barren Sarai made a mother-queen;
The promised word of God enfleshed in one
Born of a pair whose bearing days were done.

Some half-score years of fruitlessness passed by;
Then God spoke in a vision of the night:
"Fear not! I am your shield. Behold the sky —
Give number to each prick of diamond light.
Behold the countless stars of heaven bright,
For thus your offspring certainly shall be."
And once again, the son of faith found sight,
Believed the promises he could not see,
And trusted in His God, implicitly.

The Lord beheld the faith of Abram's heart,
And counted it to him as righteousness.
"I am the Lord," He said, "who set apart
This land for you to conquer and possess,
To one day fill and all the nations bless."
Still, Abram bent beneath this weight of grace:
"How will I know this favor you profess?"
To answer, He made promise in that place,
By casting Abram deep in sleep's embrace.

Behold, a dreadful darkness did descend;
The Voice, a story full of hope made known:
"Your seed with sinful nations must contend;
But then, afflicted sore and left alone,
Will rise again and come into his own."
The darkness now complete, a pillared flame
Passed through those beasts that on the ground lay prone.
"This offspring shall upon his land lay claim,
For great shall be the glory of his name."

The Lord spoke thus to Abram of his seed.
But all men, even sons of faith have doubts.
The years grown sick with hope deferred did breed
Impatient thoughts to stem the seedless drought
By human helps, though cloaked in prayers devout.
Thus Hagar bore by Abram's strength an heir.
But futile were their efforts to reroute
The path already paved to soon prepare
In empty womb, the answer to their prayer.

Another half-score years and three went by.
The Lord with Abram spoke of hope once more:
"Upon this promise made to you, rely;
Each grain of sand cast up on every shore
Could never match the matchless host I swore
Would come from you—by Abraham now known;
For nations great you hence shall see Me pour
Like water from an empty jar of stone,
From Sarah's shriveled womb bring every throne."

And it was so. The Spirit hovered o'er
The barren sea of Sarah's motherhood.
New life within her swelled; the child she bore
Like fresh creation, laughed—and it was good.
Tears streamed like rivers through a fruitful wood;
Joy filled their aching, faithful hearts with rest.
By faith the barren Sarah fears withstood,
Received pow'r to conceive; in faith confessed
Him faithful to achieve His promise blessed.

A child was born, the son of Sarah's scars;
From this old man, and him as good as dead,
Now nations great, outnumbering the stars
Would through this son shine forth, with him as head;
A fruit-filled land just as the Lord had said.
The faith of laughter filled their hearts with glee:
"Now everyone who hears that from this bed
Our Isaac came, will no doubt laugh with me!
Who would have guessed this day? Let them now see!"

But faith must through a faithful life be shown;
To trust the faithfulness of God to keep
The promises He makes in ways unknown,
Allowing Him to sow His Word and reap
The dancing joys for those who mourn and weep.
Thus Abraham was tested by the Lord.
"Arise and as you would with offered sheep,
Bind Isaac fast, your only son, with cords
And offer up to Me his blood outpoured."

So Abraham obeyed the Lord's command:
His only son on altar-wood did place
Atop a mountain in Moriahland.
He trusted that, if killed, this son of grace
Would rise again. The promise thus embraced,
He raised his knife—but Heaven stayed the stroke;
The Lord supplied a ram, his son replaced,
And in this faith-filled man fresh hope awoke:
Through death, Death's own decree He would revoke.

Day Four—Moses—Holiness

The seed, once planted, soon began to grow.
As one by one the stars each evening rise
And join the host midst twilight's fading glow,
Twelve tribes grew bright, set in Egyptian skies.
Now, Pharaoh feared this nation, feared its size;
Enslaved them, forced upon them bitter tears.
But high above, their Father heard their cries,
And so a child was born beneath that sphere,
A son to shelter them from every fear.

Protected by the midwives' holy lies
And set apart within an ark of reeds,
(Both acts of war, and faithful in God's eyes)
A fearless princess drew him from the weeds.
She took him as her son, and soon agreed
To let his mother nurse till he had grown.
Returning then to Pharaoh's house a seed,
He was in Egypt's royal palace sown;
The deeds his hand would bring as yet unknown.

Thus Moses lived a prince full forty years,
Was trained in all the wisdom of his age
And mighty grew, a first among his peers.
But soon it came into his heart to gauge
The burdens of his kin. And filled with rage
At seeing a fellow Hebrew sore oppressed,
Being all alone, he gave the guard sin's wage.
But when his brothers scorned instead of blessed,
He fled in faith, evading sure arrest.

Another forty years in exile passed.
The seed and star of Levi kept his sheep,
When some strange wonder soon his gaze held fast:
A bush consumed in flame—a holy heap
Of holy heat—and yet, each leaf did keep;
Each branch unhurt—itself but more, not less.
Before this blinding Sun, on Sinai's steep,
The lesser star sunk down in great distress.
The Light from deeper spheres the star addressed:

"Make bare your feet; you stand on holy ground.
I am the God your fathers feared and heard
In holy faith; I them with promise crowned.
Their sons I claim, in Egypt now interred;
Through you will come to them this promised word:
Their sufferings I see, their tears I keep,
Their deep affliction has my anger stirred.
I now have come, no longer will I sleep;
What weeping graves have sown, my joy will reap.

"Before your fathers were I AM. I AM:
The Living God, of living men asleep
In Sheol's bed, the God of Abraham,
Of Isaac, Jacob; now of them that weep.
I come, salvation in My hand, to sweep
Through captive lands, My own to bring to life.
In sending you I come, a vow to keep;
To take from Egypt's side a bone, a wife,
To mother stars and sand, to end all strife."

This Moses, once rejected by his kin,
Returned with power Heaven only knew.
A hardened Pharaoh, wasted in his sin;
A hardened people, Heaven's anger slew.
The gods of Egypt Moses overthrew
With blood and frogs, gnats, flies and cattle-death;
In boils and hail and locusts ripping through;
In days of darkness, thick as ashen breath;
And then, to end all plagues, their firstborn's death.

The hardened Pharaoh, given every chance
To let God's people go, to let them leave,
Destroyed his nation with his foolish stance.
Thus in I AM's own time, upon the eve
Of Exodus, the death angel that grieved
Egyptian parents sore, passed over those
Who with both bloodied post and frame believed,
Receiving life the lamb in death bestows,
Perceiving I AM's pow'r in living prose.

Thus out from Egypt God did call His son,
And led them to the cliffs that framed the sea.
But bitter Pharaoh, furious as one
Who lost his kingdom, chased them recklessly.
The people lost in fear, no time to flee,
Turned back and longed for Egypt's open grave.
They cherished now their past captivity,
Rejecting all God's promises to save,
Their hearts as hard as each cliff-pounding wave.

But God. Then Moses spoke, "Now silent be!
The Lord will fight your war." He stretched his hand:
A strong east wind blew fierce above the sea,
And sundered waves in two, revealing land;
The Most High spoke, and made the water stand.
The people, wrapped in God's own storm-black cloud,
Passed through the channels of the sea and sand.
The heavens thundered on the heads unbowed
Of Pharaoh's frenzied host, both dark and proud.

The sky grew thick with clouds, the sea with blood;
Earth rocked, and reeled, and quaked in depths unknown.
Beneath the cresting wave of death's own flood,
Both horse and rider soon were pitched and thrown —
They found the deepening depths like any stone.
The holy heavens bowed, He took His son.
Drawn out of many waters, he was shown
The mighty hand of God, the vict'ry won;
The hardened Pharaoh drowned, his host undone.

The Lord through Moses spoke once more: "Give ear!
What I have brought on Egypt, you have seen;
And how on eagles' wings I brought you here.
Now, hear my voice, obey my words, be clean!
If you will keep the covenant between
Myself and you, my treasure you shall be.
Of all the nations, you shall be my queen;
A priestly kingdom set apart and free,
A holy nation for the world to see."

But they refused to see, refused to hear.
Behind the pillared Flame and rising Cloud,
They wandered blind, in selfishness-turned-fear,
While bitter grievance left their heads unbowed,
Their hearts, like Pharaoh's host, both dark and proud.
They longed to turn to bread the desert stone;
They tested God, not trusting what He vowed;
They sought the lords in foreign lands enthroned.
And yet, I AM refused to leave His own.

Interlude—Balaam's Star

Beneath bright heaven's tutelage and song —
A mother's love—this darkened world grew weak.
The dome of heaven sang; her lessons speak
A language known, but from her gleaming throng,
Her diamond choir, on deafened ears they fell.
His heart dead to the music of the spheres,
The darkened world refused his mother's tears
And turned his tickled ears upon the hell
Of shrieking noise, which serves his baser need.
The clean, clear notes of heaven bright still shine;
Her song is rest, and yet we still confine
Ourselves beneath a canopy of screed.

Oh Star of Jacob, rise! And in your fire
Reforge our ears to hear that herald choir!

Day Five—Joshua—Courage

The stars of Abraham, and Sarah's sand,
Through deserts wandered, watered by the Rock,
And fed with birds and bread from heaven's hand.
Like quail themselves, the children swarmed and flocked
About the desert, doomed by God to walk —
Unwearied sandals worn by weary feet.
For they rejected honeyed lands and balked
At titans, whose iniquities complete
Had made them ripe to suffer swift defeat.

But 'neath the wings of Moses rose a son.
In Egypt born, the child grew strong and wise.
The fertile promised lands, as yet unwon,
This faithful man had seen with faith-filled eyes.
And so, he would the Canaanites baptize
With flame, the piercing bite of holy swords,
With trumpet blasts, the warriors' battle cries.
His enemies, beneath God's wrath outpoured,
Would fall, splayed out before the holy Lord.

When Moses' star diminished in the west,
The host of Heaven's Captain came, and spoke:
"Arise, O Joshua—these plains possessed
Of Nephilim await your sword's swift stroke;
Go, purify your lands with fire and smoke.
Be strong, fresh courage take, with you I stand;
Do not stray, nor my jealousy provoke,
But faithful be to all that I command.
For when I fight for you, none can withstand.

"The lines of your inheritance are fair:
Euphrates banks unto the Great West Sea —
A beautiful bequest I freely share
With my own son, from slavery set free.
Again, courageous, strong and fearless be;
For neither will I leave, nor e're forsake
My holy nation in their jubilee.
Arise, and crush the head of Canaan's snake,
And watch as I this promised land remake."

The Lord's own Spirit braced this man with might,
With wisdom filled, to lead the people on;
They camped beyond the river, within sight
Of lands their faithless parents had forgone.
"Prepare your stores," he said. "Come the third dawn
We pass o'er Jordan, claiming as our own
The honeyed soil that once had been withdrawn,
But now is freely given us alone.
The Lord before us goes, upon His throne."

The priests set foot on Jordan's rugged bank;
Though harvest waters rushed and overflowed,
They stood in heaps, allowing rank on rank
Of Israel's host to cross the new-formed road;
In confidence, across dry land, they strode.
Then Jericho, and every west-sea king
Of Canaan heard—the Lord before them rode.
Their spirits failed, like winter snow in spring,
Their heart's own courage fast abandoning.

Soon evening came, when Joshua beheld
A Man, and fell before His majesty.
He spoke as one who with one word expelled
The fallen hosts of hell in victory:
"I Am commander of the Lord's army,
And now have come. You stand on holy ground;
Make bare your feet, and hear what you shall see.
Proud Jericho—in wanton lusts unbound —
Their ruin will through Canaan quick resound."

The strategy received, war was begun.
For six days, seven priests with seven horns
Before the ark, with every man as one
Behind the Lord, marched round beneath the scorn
Of that city, in silence, as was sworn.
Alone, the trumpets charged the tightened air.
Then Jacob's hosts arose that seventh morn
And seven times marched round that stone-clad lair,
Then stopped, a cry upon their lips—a prayer.

At once, triumphant trumpeting shot through
That anxious air with Heaven's force behind!
Let loose like arrows feather-fletched and true.
A shout broke out! Their courage-cries entwined
With trumpet blasts in I AM's hand combined
To wreck a wreckage utter and complete.
The wall of Jericho, like an old rind
Being cut away, lay wasted in defeat;
Down, downward fast it fell, like sickled wheat.

Each breathing life was killed beneath the sword,
Their blood, an offering for guilt and shame.
All things devoted to the holy Lord
To be destroyed, to purge that land with flame.
Save Rahab, and those covered by her name,
For she had covered and kept safe the spies
Who spied the land before destruction came.
This act of faith was precious in God's eyes;
He made from her a promised son to rise.

As birds have bright blue realms to wing and spread;
As seas, great beasts majestic rule and roam;
As earth and all its fullness have their head
In Him who gives all governors a home —
From darkened depths to heaven's brightest dome —
So too this promised land He gave His son:
Twelve tribes, inheriting the Canaan loam
To sanctify with worship of the One,
To work and rest, their slaving days now done.

But hands that work apart from hearts that trust
Refuse to find their joy in given rest.
For envy drives men back into the dust
And curdles chests that courage once possessed.
The tribes that flooded Jordan's banks—oppressed
By fears and failing hearts; pale souls grown thin —
They failed to drive out Canaan from their nests.
Thus conquerors were conquered from within
And lost the promised lands in grievous sin.

They turned to worship gods unknown and new,
Rejecting all the signs and wonders seen.
With hearts of dust, they lusted after stew
While birthrights offered fields of fertile green,
Full streams of water rushing pure and clean.
With hearts as dark and cold as any grave,
The seed descended into depths obscene.
Their only hope: to call on Him they crave —
A Father quick with mercy, quick to save.

Day Six—David—Humility

Unyielding seed, grown fruitless in the land,
Exploiting others as each eye deemed right,
Waxed fat in lust and kicked against the hand
That showered blessings undeserved, despite
Declaring their "amens" which did invite
God's curse for every God-forsaking crime.
Relentless cycles—peace, fall, war, and flight;
Repentance, rescue, tempered for a time;
But soon engorged again on passion's grime.

In answer to this faithless fattening
A promised child, a son was set apart;
Out of the dust of sheep God formed a king
In His own image, after His own heart.
Unto this son the Spirit would impart
An everlasting throne, on which would reign
An everlasting king—a faithful start,
Inevitably flawed and filled with pain,
Would end in perfect peace, worldwide domain.

Still green, this shoot of Jesse left his flock
To find his brothers cowering before
Goliath—gnarled of heart, and like a rock
In size and strength; this Philistine brought war
On Israel's thin-souled host, would loudly roar
Crass blasphemies, and hold their courage cheap.
The humble shepherd's shame could not ignore
The giant's scornful swagger sown to reap
Swift death—the honor of the Lord to keep.

With five smooth stones, a sling, and simple trust
Young David stood before that witless brute —
For that was all he saw beneath the crust
Of mockeries, defiances, thick suits
Of armor—reckless piece of Cain-born fruit.
"Am I a dog?" the canine cried in scorn.
But David spoke, "No more will you pollute
God's clean and wholesome air with threats stillborn.
Your neck will know my sword, and soon be shorn."

Goliath rose but, ready-sling in hand,
Young David fast let fly the stoney ball
And struck the brute between the eyes as planned.
The giant—like a tower, like a wall —
Fell down, from dust to dust, in David's thrall;
He took the dog's own sword and with one blow
Removed the mocker's head, and gave to Saul
The host of fallen Philistines laid low,
Cold corpses gathered for the hawk and crow.

Thus David grew, gained favor in the land:
"A thousand Saul struck down; ten thousand more
Has David conquered by his mighty hand."
While praise on women's lips, an open sore
On Saul's embittered mind. The weak king swore
He never would relent till David's head
Was severed from its place. Ironic war
Between the savior and the saved soon spread
Across the wilderness, where David fled.

Still faithful to the Lord's anointed king,
Though hunted from each hill and barren cave,
The man with God's own heart began to sing:
Of pain and peace, of trials and the grave,
A breathless longing for the Lord to save.
His prayers, attuned to heaven's melody,
Brought air beneath the suffocating wave,
Gave life to limbs bereft of liberty,
And planted faith beside the watered tree.

With eyes aflame, affixed on Heaven's Word,
Humility grows fierce, tenacious, bold;
It wrestles faithfully with hope deferred,
It argues for the promises of old,
It does not rest until, His name extolled,
The righteousness of Heaven bears much fruit.
Humility will God alone behold;
On self is silent—fleshly thoughts are moot;
A simple trust in soil, a nurtured root.

Soon Saul, in judgment fell, in Sheol slept,
And David ascended the promised throne.
Anointed as a youth, he did accept
The heavy burden—then as yet unknown —
To wait through troubled years till time had grown
Complete in Heaven's mind to crown him king.
The Lord, His mind, to David then made known:
"When to your grave your bones they bring
A kingdom will I build from your offspring.

"That son from your own loins shall reign in peace.
His hands shall build a house to hold My Name;
His governance once fixed shall never cease.
But when upon his shoulders comes the shame
Your sin conceives, and when he takes the blame,
Then with the stripes of men he must endure
The wrath iniquity deserves upon his frame.
But know, my steadfast love will prove most sure,
Your throne eternal will remain secure."

Thus humble hearts content must be to rest,
And fix their eyes on Him who forms the soul.
But David's sight grew dim. With swelling chest
And lust inflamed, he grasped and stole
Uriah's wife, of his life took control
And sent him to his death, in blinding heat.
But with this hellish feat he swallowed whole
The sin which death alone could now complete,
And lost the infant child of his deceit.

With that thin thread a woven tapestry
Unraveled in the palace of the king.
For sin, as ripples on the water flee
The sunken rock, spreads fast; it makes of spring
A winter where, beneath the ice and sting
Of death, all stone-cold passions are pursued.
In exile, David stricken down took wing;
His pride by age and folly now subdued,
The bitter days of consequence ensued.

Day Seven—Solomon—Wisdom

With humbled, broken heart, the seed returned
To reign in peace throughout his final days —
The faithfulness of Him whose grace, unearned,
Flows freely down on hearts transfixed in praise,
Restored salvation's joy to trust His ways.
Still, David's hands, imbrued with blood and war,
Could not achieve his heart's desire—to raise
A house to hold God's name, to come before
The Presence there, His beauty to adore.

But Faithfulness again the shepherd blessed:
A promised child was born, a sabbath son —
A king to bring both lasting rule and rest.
And so, when David slept, his Solomon
Ascended to the throne, the kingdom won:
Euphrates' banks unto the Great West Sea.
All lesser kings and lands beneath the sun
Did tribute bring, to bow on bended knee
And render homage in humility.

Now Jacob's seed was as the stars and sand,
The promise made to Abraham come true,
It seemed. The nations now throughout the land
Were blessed—their gold as common as the dew,
Their silver flowed in streams the kingdom through.
The people daily feasted on the best;
Vast tables, fit for kings, the common knew;
Each man beneath his vine and fig tree blessed,
The promised son enthroned, the land at rest.

Soon, David's deep desire took shape in stone,
In cedar, cyprus, olivewood, and gold,
Engraved with flowers, fruits, and palms full-grown,
Each surface overlaid with wealth untold;
Strong pillars kept the doors like men of old;
Carved cherubim descended from on high,
Like gleaming shadows cast in heaven's mold,
In silent peals of thunder, rending sky
And heaven's floor—a second Mount Sinai.

The House was built; the heavens bowed; He came.
Within the curtained womb, the cloud took form;
In holy darkness throned the pillared Flame,
Descending glory from outside the swarm
Of stars, inhabiting the thunder's storm.
The One who spoke creation into being
Creation now enclosed in shadow-form.
The Presence sat on cherubs' outstretched wing,
And spoke this word to Solomon the king:

"My son, your prayers and pleas of heart are heard.
I holy make this house with my own Name,
To hold within my eyes, my heart, my Word;
A house for every nation to proclaim
In prayer and praise the glories of my fame.
My son, now walk in faith before my sight
As David walked, and honor me the same;
Obey my words, and keep along the light,
And I will give your sons your father's right."

But Solomon was not so strong a son.
Though wiser king the world has never known,
And richer too, his faith grew small, undone
By wine and wives, the power of his throne,
By grasping after all this world had shown.
Beneath creation's lamp, no hope was found
To fill with life an empty heart of stone,
To anchor purpose to putrescent ground,
To know the gain of being the sovereign crowned.

And so the king of rest did restless grow,
Chasing the embers of a dying sun.
But faith, if faith at all, will always know
And cause, before that final day is done
Hearts to remember: He, the Lord, is One.
That memory gives light to understand
Our purpose, place, and posture as a son
Of Him Who was and is—that by His hand
We love and laugh and drink the fruitful land.

So came this final creed of that wise king:
"What is this mist, this fleeting breath, this cloud?
All life is dust, borne high upon wind's wing;
What gain therefore has man beneath this shroud,
The solid tombstone time that falls unbowed
Upon the broken backs of beasts and men?
The world, a field of weariness unplowed —
For that which came before will be again;
And that which came before will be again.

For nothing new can be beneath the sun;
Yet fools and men refuse to rest content
With how creation turns beneath the One
Who shapes each passing moment with intent
And fills each heart with heaven's undying scent.
For all God does endures beyond time's frame,
And none can plumb what God Himself has bent.
For decades I have seen the fool seek fame,
To try, in vain, to leave a lasting name.

So this is all: to eat and drink and love;
Beneath the hand of Him Who is, we rest.
True wisdom, music of the spheres above,
Descends and bids us join Deep Heaven's fest,
To see above the sun a higher quest.
For nature cries and yearns for something more;
Alone, it dies; life hastens, unpossessed.
But eyes of faith see coming on time's shore
True Food—Him Whom this famished world is for."

Interlude—The World Unmade

Seven shadows lengthened toward the rising eastern night.
Kings and priests had given into pagan sacrifice
While the pillared Flame, behind the curtain, out of sight,
Patiently bore with His blood-stained children's wanton vice.
He sent prophets, speaking hard truth, severe love and grace,
Calling out with arms wide open, "Without cost or price,
Come and buy! Come all who starve and thirst to my embrace!
Without money, eat and drink my bread and wine and live.
Oh, why feast on what will not the emptiness efface?"

Elijah first, true worship to restore, took captive
The restless host of Baal, with fire from holy heaven
And put them to the sword, the children to forgive.

Elisha then, with double-portioned power, men
Restored to life and healthy limb, to work and keep
The land in gratitude from love begotten.

Isaiah soon, beneath the wing's rushing sweep,
Fell down before the One with authority,
And preached the child whose government runs deep.

Jeremiah warned the kings what would be;
He begged the stars to fall before the sun,
To trust their God in captivity.

Daniel, too, obedient to none
But Him who, like a rock, fills the earth,
Spoke courage to the exiled son.

Ezekiel foresaw new birth
As waters flowed down from above
Making fresh each salty firth.

Malachi, the last to love,
Saw light shine—the darkness done —
The dawn-descending dove:

The rising righteous Sun.

Day Eight—Jesus—Love

The world descended into silent dust.
Four hundred journeys round that sphere of light —
Which like a warrior runs his race, robust
With joy—no vision saw, no second sight
Received from Heaven's hand, no word to write.
Blind world—unmade by sin and selfish men
Who would despise their only hope despite
Old paths uncovered time and time again.
It looked the world would end in night. But then:

The Spirit hovered once more o'er the deep;
"Let there be Light" once more rang loud and clear.
This Light, the light and life of men, would reap
The harvest halting shadows proved was near;
The seventh seventh Jubilee now here.
For God Himself had from the pillared flame
Descended even further from that sphere.
Who Earth and Heaven named, He took a name;
Creator of all things, a thing became.

Within the quiet of a virgin womb,
At one time formless, fresh and new,
That Seed of light was sown sans earthly groom.
The Word, the *Arche* formed in flesh, broke through
Naphtali's night—their promised light come true.
Within an earthly spec, eternal span,
Within created flesh the Maker grew,
Within that formless womb a world began;
Within a woman, God was made a Man.

The Infinite as infant child was nursed;
In awe, His mother's husband spoke His name:
Jesus, David's Son—sent to save the cursed.
The suckled Word, upon His mother's frame
Soon slept, despising every earthly shame.
But these are wonders far beyond our ken,
A world too wild for lines of ink to tame;
Our minds too small and weak, our infant pen
Too frail to fully capture God with men.

The Seed matured beneath the Father's love;
His patience, wisdom, joy, like fruit full grown.
Thus, rising from the stream, the Holy Dove
Descended on His shoulder, making known
The Father's perfect pleasure in His own.
From broken water, Living Water swelled;
"Let it be so, for righteousness alone,"
He said to John, that desert voice compelled
To make way for the Lamb his hands now held.

Thence, God's Son to the wilderness did go,
Alone with thirst and hunger forty days
And forty nights, our weaknesses to know.
The devil, hoping here by cunning ways
To fell the Son of Man, before Him raised
Three tempting words to try His confidence.
True Israel repelled each lie, ablaze
With faith in what was written—sure defense
Against the serpent's every sly pretense.

Now victory began—the fall reversed;
The serpent's lies rejected out of hand,
And life restored to the unclean and cursed:
Blind men began to see, the lame to stand,
Broken men made fit for worship, the land
Made whole and holy—healing of the scars.
For Satan fell from Heaven with his band
Of fallen angels, fallen morning stars,
Like lightening cold and spent—a conquered Mars.

To tell the tribes the Kingdom now was here,
By Him, twelve men ambassadors became,
With seventy to follow. Far and near
They roamed with courage, making whole the lame,
Subjecting demons to His mighty name.
Authority to govern was His right —
A right he laid aside to take the shame
Of broken man, to bring us living light;
But He would rise, his enemies to smite.

He set His face, and sought Jerusalem.
For this was why Immanuel was born:
A second Adam, shoot from Jesse's stem,
Returned to dust in death, in thistle-thorn—
World-weight of sin upon His shoulders borne.
And so the Son of Man to Zion went,
His head, a crown of curses would adorn.
Humility, with cross and shame content,
To sacrifice would willingly assent.

Now see Him there—the silent shape of Love.
His purpose kept, He rests upon the tree.
A vision of wisdom; eyes fixed above,
His gaze beyond the shame; He patiently
Awaits His final breath—our jubilee —
His Spirit free from bitterness and pride.
On gopher-wood the Son of God would be
The truest act of worship, and provide
Our sabbath-shaped redemption. Jesus died.

What paradox of feelings these words bring!
To feel the weight of shame that made it so,
And still to lift our heads and boldly sing
Redemption songs from hearts that freely flow
With gratitude, renewed by blood to know
A world made new—hearts reconciled and free!
For to the cross of Jesus we must go
To die, down to His grave on bended knee.
O Death, where is thy sting, thy victory?

He shepherds us through the valley of death
With strong but gentle hands—the way is low —
And by His Spirit gives us Heaven's Breath.
Our fears, dark whispers of the fallen foe
Who tries to shift our eyes from what we know,
Upon that bloody cross with Him have died.
Thus, in these shadowlands He does bestow
Fresh courage, strength, and boldness to His bride,
We who were taken from His riven side.

Within the womb of earth three days He slept,
His body dead, forsaken in the grave;
His followers in fear—the women wept.
The stone rolled before the mouth of the cave.
But on the eighth morn, when the dawn's first wave
Of light fell on that stone, and shook the earth,
The Seed was raised to life, the cursed to save.
Then all of Heaven shook with eager mirth:
The womb of Adam's death had given birth.

A new humanity—a world reborn;
The seven shadows' shape in Jesus found.
To setting of the sun from rising morn,
All points to Him, the Sovereign Son now crowned —
To Him let all creation now their songs resound!
The Child is born, now reigns the promised king;
The Son is giv'n, all knees must find the ground;
All winters come, redemption songs now sing,
For Jesus is the resurrected Spring.

Epilogue

The world begins again; on Heaven's cloud
The Son of Man ascended to His throne
To sit until His enemies avowed
That Jesus Christ was King, and He alone:
His name above all names, the cornerstone
That over every nation reigns with might.
The earth itself beneath sin's weight now groans
In eager expectation of our right
Revealed, as children fixed in His delight.

His first decree: to send the Comforter.
Like Sinai wreathed in rushing wind and flame,
The upper room on Pentecost, astir
With Spirit wind and tongues of fire, became
The house that held God's holy name.
The dawn-descending Dove with healing grace,
Transforms His heirs into a breathing frame
In which the pillared Flame can place
Himself, to birth a new and holy race.

Therefore, O nations! Lift your voice and sing!
A race transformed—by Heaven's Bard well fed —
Must words of Truth and lives of Beauty bring
Each day, before our good and faithful Head
To be reshaped by Gospel wine and bread;
The memory on which we feast is strong.
In this, to understanding love is wed,
To worship Him within the holy throng,
To sing aloud our own redemption song.

Gratitude

A warm word of thanks for Messrs. Schwager and O'Donnell for their time, encouragement, and grammatical mastery.

Also to my Uncle Ric, who helped give Day Seven the direction it needed.

You can join the Jovial Press email list and see the rest of our catalog, including more books by Joe Carlson, at www.jovial-pub.com

Joseph Carlson, a graduate of New St. Andrews College, is a teaching elder at Trinity Bible Church in Felton, California. Both he and his wife look forward to one day moving to Narnia. He can be found scrawling around on the world wide web at joecarlson.net.

Made in the USA
Las Vegas, NV
20 December 2023

83263957R00038